Beginner's Guide to
Knitting in the Round

LEISURE ARTS, INC. • Maumelle, Arkansas

For beginners who are ready to advance beyond flat knitting, working in the round is a natural progression, says designer Kristin Omdahl. "It alleviates a lot of seams," she explains, "which gives a better structure to your projects, as well as making them more pleasing aesthetically." Kristin created the designs in this book to be easy projects for learning several methods of working in the round, as well as favorite family gifts.

Working in the round is easier than you think, especially with our step-by-step instructions and free online videos (watch for 🎥 camera icons throughout the book).

Knitting in the round is achieved by using circular needles or double pointed needles. For each method, we'll teach you how to use the needles and give you a few easy projects to practice your new skills.

After you learn these two methods, a third section is devoted to combination projects that teach you how to transition from one type of needle to the other. This comes in handy as your number of stitches increases or decreases, since circular needles can hold lots of stitches, but double pointed needles are needed for small stitch counts.

As you knit in the round, you form a tube-like continuous fabric and work each round without turning. A welcome advantage of this is that stockinette stitch becomes super easy, accomplished simply by knitting every round. You'll wish everything could be knitted in the round! Enjoy learning!

Meet the Designer

Founder of StyledByKristin.com and design company KRISTIN, Kristin Omdahl designs knit and crochet garments and patterns and is the author of numerous pattern books and magazine articles. She was the crochet expert for 10 seasons on Knitting Daily TV on public television, and she conducts seminars on crochet around the country. Passionate about design, Kristin is inspired by textures and geometric shapes found in nature. She enjoys knitting and crocheting in her orchid garden in sunny Southwest Florida.

24

10

28

6

13

32

17

35

GETTING STARTED

How to Use This Book

The best way to learn to knit in the round is to start with a simple project and build your skills a little at a time. In this book, we start with the easiest projects for each type of needle and then give you projects that let you practice those skills and pick up additional knowledge. To learn about using circular needles, begin with the Headband on page 6. Then continue practicing with circular needles to make the Cowl and Lace Capelet. If you prefer to learn about using double pointed needles first, begin with the little Pouch on page 17. Then continue using double pointed needles for the Baby Hat and Fingerless Mitts.

Our instructions for both types of needles take you step by step, so your learning experience is sure to be successful! We've even created free online videos found at www.leisurearts.com/6342 to help you; orange camera icons 📹 throughout the book let you know when there are videos to watch.

Besides teaching you all about using circular needles and double pointed needles, this book also explains when it is best to use each type and how to transition from one to the other. For example, circular needles can hold lots of stitches, but a set of double pointed needles is needed for small stitch counts. Sometimes, you will have to begin a project using one type of needle and change to the other type when the stitch count increases or decreases (such as for the Family Hat on page 32 and the Baby Blanket on page 35). But don't worry — we'll walk you through the process with ease!

Supplies

There are two types of needles used to knit in the round - circular needles *(page 5)* and double pointed needles *(page 16)*.

A shopping list is provided with each project that lets you know which type of needles to use. Markers are used to indicate the beginning of the rounds. Since gauge is crucial to the success of some of the projects, you'll want a tape measure. A yarn needle or tapestry needle is used to weave in yarn ends.

CIRCULAR NEEDLES

Circular needles consist of two short needles joined by a flexible cable that comes in various lengths.

Circular needles are ideal when knitting large tubes such as a tote bag or sweater body or when you have too many stitches for double pointed needles. (They can also be used for flat knitting worked in rows.)

Types
Circular needles come in bamboo, wood, metal, plastic, or with coated tips.

Needle Length
The length of the entire needle (including tips and cable) should be at least 2" (5 cm) shorter than the circumference of the piece being knit. Circular needles come in many lengths and needle sizes. Sets with detachable tips and cables are also available, providing an endless combination of needle sizes and cable lengths to adapt to your needs.

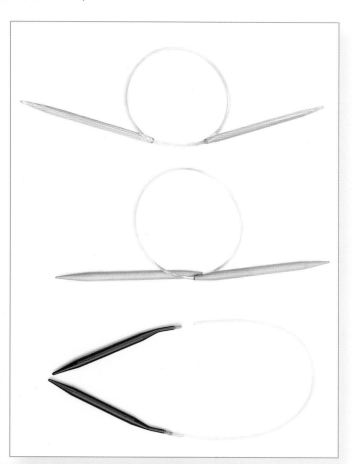

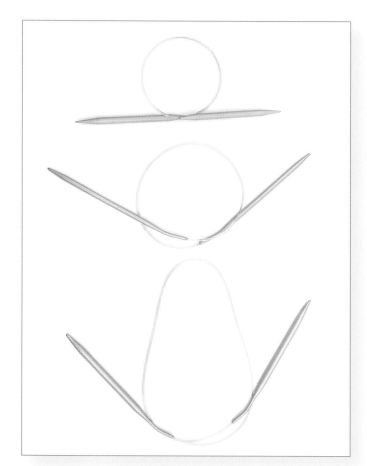

HEADBAND

 **EASY**

This is a quick beginner project that uses a nicely textured stitch pattern but doesn't require any shaping. You'll need a circular needle to make the adult size, but the child's size requires double pointed needles because it has fewer stitches.

Finished Adult Size: 4" wide x 18" circumference (10 cm x 45.5 cm)

Note: A child's size, 3" wide x 16" circumference (7.5 cm x 40.5 cm), must be made with double pointed needles. See page 9 for instructions.

SHOPPING LIST

Yarn (Medium Weight)

[3.5 ounces, 280 yards
(100 grams, 256 meters) per skein]:

☐ 1 skein

Knitting Needles

Adult size:

☐ 16" (40.5 cm) Circular, size 8 (5 mm)
or size needed for gauge

Child's size:

☐ 7-8" (18-20.5 cm) Double pointed (set of 5),
size 8 (5 mm) **or** size needed for gauge

Additional Supplies

Adult size:

☐ Marker - ring style, split ring, or scrap yarn

Child's size:

☐ Split ring marker

GAUGE INFORMATION

In pattern, working in rows,

16 sts = 4" (10 cm)

Gauge Swatch: 3½" (9 cm) wide

Cast on 14 sts.

Row 1: K1, ★ (K, YO, K) all in next st, P3; repeat from ★ 2 times **more**, K1: 20 sts.

Row 2: P1, K3 tog, (P3, K3 tog) twice, P4: 14 sts.

Row 3: K1, ★ P3, (K, YO, K) all in next st; repeat from ★ 2 times **more**, K1: 20 sts.

Row 4: P4, K3 tog, (P3, K3 tog) twice, P1: 14 sts.

Rows 5-8: Repeat Rows 1-4.

Bind off all sts.

TECHNIQUES USED

📹 (K, YO, K) all in next stitch *(Fig. 21, page 44)*
📹 K3 tog *(Fig. 23, page 45)*
📹 P3 tog *(Fig. 29, page 47)*

INSTRUCTIONS
Using a Circular Needle

ADULT'S SIZE

Using a circular needle, cast on 72 sts.

🎥◀ **Place a marker** on the right hand point to indicate the beginning of the round *(Fig. 1)*. You may use a purchased ring, a split ring marker, or a loop of a contrasting color scrap yarn *(see Markers, page 41)*.

Fig. 1

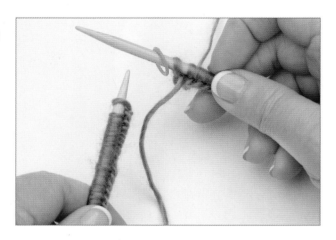

🎥 **Straighten the stitches** on the needle to be sure that the cast on ridge lies on the inside of the needle and is not twisted around the needle *(Fig. 2)*.

Fig. 2

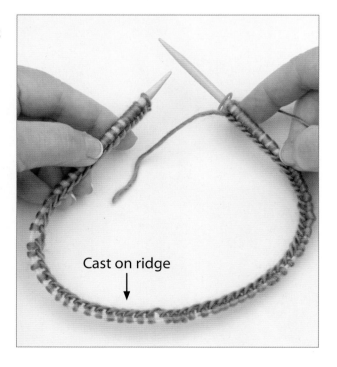

Cast on ridge

Rnd 1: 🎥◀ **To begin working in the round**, hold the needle so that the skein of yarn is attached to the stitch closest to the right hand point and knit across the stitches on the left hand point *(Fig. 3)*. Continue knitting each stitch until you reach the marker.

Fig. 3

You will work around the outside of the Headband with the **right** side facing. Continue working each round without turning the work.

When you reach the marker on each round, slip it from the left point to the right point.

Fabrics: The top and bottom borders are worked in Garter Stitch. When working in the round, this fabric is made the opposite of how it is made when working in rows. To form Garter Stitch, knit one round, purl one round. To form Stockinette Stitch, knit every round.

Rnd 2: Purl around.

Rnd 3: Knit around.

Rnd 4: Purl around.

Rnd 5: ★ (K, YO, K) all in next st, P3; repeat from ★ around: 108 sts.

Rnd 6: (K3, P3 tog) around: 72 sts.

Rnd 7: ★ P3, (K, YO, K) all in next st; repeat from ★ around: 108 sts.

Rnd 8: (P3 tog, K3) around: 72 sts.

Repeat Rnds 5-8 until Headband measures approximately 3¹/₂" (9 cm) from cast on edge, ending by working Rnd 6 or Rnd 8.

Last 4 Rnds: Repeat Rnds 3 and 4, twice.

Bind off all sts **loosely**.

GOOD JOB!!!
You completed your first project knitting in the round on circular needles!

CHILD'S SIZE
Due to the small number of stitches, double pointed needles are required (*see Double Pointed Needles, page 16*).

Using a double pointed needle, cast on 64 sts.

📹 **Divide sts onto 4 needles** (*Fig. 11, page 30*), placing 16 sts on each needle and form a square. 📹 Place a split ring marker around the first stitch to indicate the beginning of the round (*see Markers, page 41*).

Work same as Adult size until Headband measures approximately 2¹/₂" (6.5 cm) from cast on edge, ending by working Rnd 6 or Rnd 8.

Last 4 Rnds: Repeat Rnds 3 and 4, twice.

Bind off all sts **loosely**.

COWL

 EASY

A large circular needle and super bulky yarn make this project extra quick to knit. You'll have fun watching the ripples take shape, too!

Finished Size: 19¹/₂" (49.5 cm) circumference

──────── SHOPPING LIST ────────

Yarn (Super Bulky Weight)
[2.8 ounces, 77 yards
(80 grams, 70 meters) per skein]:
☐ Main Color - 1 skein
☐ Contrasting Color - 20 yards
   (18.5 meters)

Knitting Needles
☐ 16" (40.5 cm) Circular, size 10¹/₂ (6.5 mm)
   or size needed for gauge

Additional Supplies
☐ Marker - ring style, split ring, or
   scrap yarn

GAUGE INFORMATION

In pattern,
   1 repeat (12 sts) = 3¹/₄" (8.25 cm)

TECHNIQUES USED

🎥 YO (*Fig. 16a, page 42*)
🎥 (K, YO, K) all in next stitch (*Fig. 21, page 44*)
🎥 Slip 2, K1, P2SSO (*Fig. 27, page 46*)

INSTRUCTIONS
BODY

With Contrasting Color, cast on 72 sts.

▶ Place a marker on the right hand point to indicate the beginning of the round. You may use a purchased ring, split ring marker, or a length of contrasting color yarn *(see Markers, page 41)*.

▶ Straighten the stitches on the needle to be sure that the cast on ridge lies on the inside of the needle and is not twisted around the needle *(Fig. 2, page 8)*.

Hold the needle so that the skein of yarn is attached to the stitch closest to the right hand point and work around the outside of the Cowl with the **right** side facing.

Rnd 1: ★ K9, slip 2, K1, P2SSO; repeat from ★ around: 60 sts.

Rnd 2: Remove marker, K1, place marker to change beginning of rnd, K3, (K, YO, K) all in next st, ★ K9, (K, YO, K) all in next st; repeat from ★ around to last 6 sts, K6: 72 sts.

Rnd 3: Slip marker, ★ K9, slip 2, K1, P2SSO; repeat from ★ around: 60 sts.

Cut Contrasting Color. Using Main Color, repeat Rnds 2 and 3 until Cowl measures approximately 5" (12.5 cm) from bottom of ripple on cast on edge, ending by working Rnd 3.

Cut Main Color; with Contrasting Color, repeat Rnds 2 and 3 once.

Bind off all sts loosely in pattern.

We've created bonus videos for you @ www.leisurearts.com/6342

Take a look!

LACE CAPELET

 INTERMEDIATE

This project involves changing to a longer circular needle after you finish the ribbed cowl and increase the number of stitches to start the lace body.

Finished Size: 14½" high x 44" circumference at bottom edge (37 cm x 112 cm)

SHOPPING LIST

Yarn (Fine Weight)
[3 ounces, 498 yards
(85 grams, 455 meters) per skein]:
☐ 1 skein

Knitting Needles
Circular, size 8 (5 mm):
☐ 16" (40.5 cm) **and**
☐ 24" (61 cm) **or** size needed for gauge

Additional Supplies
☐ Marker - ring style, split ring, or scrap yarn

GAUGE INFORMATION
In K6, P6 ribbing (relaxed), 12 sts = 2½" (6.25 cm)
In K4, P4 ribbing (relaxed), 8 sts = 2" (5 cm)
In lace pattern, 1 repeat (10 sts) = 2¾" (7 cm)

TECHNIQUES USED
▶ YO (*Fig. 16, page 42*)
▶ K2 tog (*Fig. 22, page 45*)
▶ Slip 1, K1, PSSO (*Figs. 25a & b, page 46*)
▶ Slip 1, K2 tog, PSSO (*Fig. 26, page 46*)
▶ P2 tog (*Fig. 28, page 47*)

INSTRUCTIONS
RIBBING

Using shorter circular needle, cast on 120 sts.

Place a marker on the right hand point to indicate the beginning of the round *(Fig. 1, page 8)*. Straighten the stitches and begin working in the round *(Figs. 2 & 3, page 8)*.

Rnd 1: (K6, P6) around.

Repeat Rnd 1 until Ribbing measures approximately 4" (10 cm) from cast on edge.

Decrease Rnd: ★ K2 tog, K2, K2 tog, P2 tog, P2, P2 tog; repeat from ★ around: 80 sts.

Next Rnd: (K4, P4) around.

Repeat last Rnd until Ribbing measures approximately 8" (20.5 cm) from cast on edge.

LACE BODY

Rnd 1 (Right side)**:** Knit around.

Work the next round with the longer needle. It is needed to accommodate all of the stitches that will be increased on Rnd 2.

Rnd 2: (YO, K1) around: 160 sts.

Rnd 3: Knit around.

Rnd 4: ★ (YO, slip 1, K1, PSSO) twice, K1, (K2 tog, YO) twice, K1; repeat from ★ around.

Rnd 5: Knit around.

Rnd 6: ★ YO, slip 1, K1, PSSO, YO, slip 1, K2 tog, PSSO, YO, K2 tog, YO, K3; repeat from ★ around.

Rnd 7: Knit around.

Repeat Rnds 4-7 until Lace Body measures approximately 10" (25.5 cm), ending by working Rnd 5 or Rnd 7.

BORDER

Rnd 1: Purl around.

Rnd 2: Knit around.

Rnds 3-5: Repeat Rnds 1 and 2 once, then repeat Rnd 1 once **more**.

Bind off all sts **loosely** in **knit**.

Fold Ribbing in half to right side to form cowl.

DOUBLE POINTED NEEDLES

Double pointed needles have a point on both ends which allow you to work in the round and are ideal when knitting small tubes such as a pouch, small hat, or socks. They are also used for working the shaping of an adult hat or the center of a large circle such as a baby blanket.

Types

Needles that are made from bamboo, wood, or any non-slippery material are nice for beginners, because the stitches stay on the needles better than other materials.

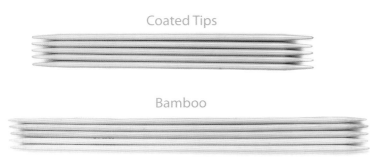

Coated Tips

Bamboo

Needle Sets

Each size of double pointed needles comes in sets of either 4 or 5 needles. One needle is to work with and the remaining needles hold the stitches. The Shopping List provided with each project will tell you how many needles are required for your project.

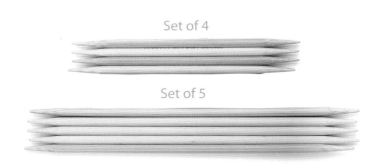

Set of 4

Set of 5

Needle Length

Double pointed needles come in various lengths. We used 5", 7", and 10" (12.5 cm, 18 cm, and 25.5 cm). The length called for in the Shopping List is based on the number of stitches that each needle will hold with the weight of the yarn used.

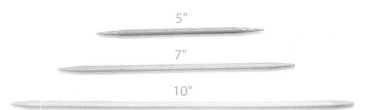

5"

7"

10"

Point Protectors

When you have more stitches on the needles than what the needles can easily hold, use point protectors to prevent the stitches from slipping off. They can also be used to keep your stitches in place if you set your project aside.

POUCH

 **EASY**

This is a great starter project for working with double pointed needles. You will learn all the basics of working with 4 needles, one of the most popular techniques for knitting in the round. You'll also learn to make an easy cord, using only 2 double pointed needles to knit a tube formed with just 3 stitches.

Finished Size: 3" wide x 6" high (7.5 cm x 15 cm)

SHOPPING LIST

Yarn (Medium Weight)
☐   55 yards (50.5 meters)

Knitting Needles
☐   5" (12.5 cm) Double pointed (set of 4),
     size 8 (5 mm) **or** size needed for gauge

Additional Supplies
☐   Split ring marker
☐   Yarn needle

GAUGE INFORMATION

Working in rows, in Stockinette Stitch (knit one row, purl one row),

   8 sts and 11 rows = 2" (5 cm)

To make a gauge swatch, use two double pointed needles.

TECHNIQUES USED
▸ YO *(Fig. 16a, page 42)*
▸ Slip 1, K1, PSSO *(Figs. 25a & b, page 46)*

INSTRUCTIONS
Using 4 Double Pointed Needles
POUCH

Beginning at the top edge, you're going to cast on all of the stitches needed for the Top Border onto one needle, then transfer a third of the stitches onto each of two more needles. Three needles will hold the stitches and the remaining needle is for working.

TIP: It's important that the cast on stitches are snug (but not tight) so that the needles won't slide out of the stitches on their own.

Cast 24 sts onto one needle.

📹 **Dividing the sts into thirds,** slip 8 sts onto each of 2 needles **purlwise** *(Fig. 4a)* leaving 8 sts on the last needle *(Fig. 4b).* Slide the sts to the center of each needle to prevent them from slipping off.

Fig. 4a

Fig. 4b

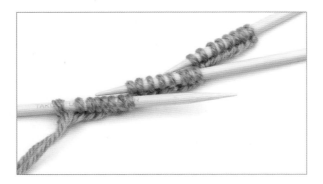

📹 **Form a triangle with the 3 needles** keeping the cast on ridge straight and not twisted around the needles *(Fig. 4c).* The third needle is the one with the working yarn attached to it.

Fig. 4c

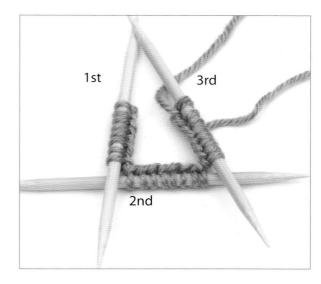

BEGIN WORKING IN ROUNDS

Rnd 1 (Right side)**:** Slide the sts on the first needle to the tip. 📹 Hold the first and third needles *(Fig. 5a).* The second needle can also be held, or it can just dangle.

Fig. 5a

Hold the needle with the yarn close to the needle you will be working across. Using the empty needle, 📹 K1 working the st firmly to prevent a gap between the needles.

Place a split ring marker around the st just made to indicate the first st *(Fig. 5b)*.

Fig. 5b

Knit across the first needle; slip the 8 sts just made to the center of the needle. You will now have an empty needle with which to work the stitches from the next needle.

As you work across a needle, the other two needles can just dangle *(Fig. 5c)*, or they can be held with your left hand *(Fig. 5d)*.

Fig. 5c

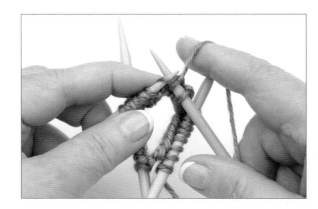

Fig. 5d

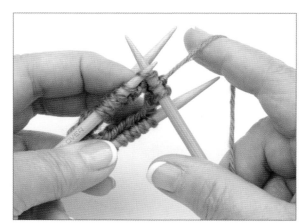

When you are ready to work across a needle, slip the sts to the tip, then back to the center of their new needle after all of the sts are worked off.

When going from one needle to the next, be careful that the working yarn comes from **under** the right hand needle and not over it as that would create an extra stitch.

★ Using the empty needle, K1 working the st firmly, knit across the needle; repeat from ★ once **more**. You should have 3 needles with 8 sts on each needle *(Fig. 5e)*.

Fig. 5e

You did it! Rest assured, holding the needles will get easier as the piece gets larger.

TIPS

TIPS

You will work around the outside of the Pouch, with the **right** side facing you.

After the second round, the stitches won't be able to twist around the needles. Just check to be sure the needles all have the **right** side facing out.

Continue working the first stitch of each needle firmly to prevent gaps that cause the **ladder effect** *(Fig. 6)*.

Fig. 6

ladder effect

At the beginning of each round, move the marker to the new stitch after the first stitch has been worked.

Fabrics: The Top and Bottom Borders are worked in Garter Stitch and the Body is worked in Stockinette Stitch. When working in the round, these fabrics are made the opposite of how they are made when working in rows. To form the Garter Stitch Borders, knit one round, purl one round. To form the Stockinette Stitch Body, knit every round.

Rnd 2: Purl across each needle.

Rnd 3: Knit across each needle.

Rnd 4: Purl across each needle.

Rnd 5 (Eyelet rnd): ★ K2, YO, slip 1, K1, PSSO; repeat from ★ around.

Now that the Top Border is complete, knit each round for the Stockinette Stitch Body until the Pouch measures approximately 5" (12.5 cm) from cast on edge.

TIP: While working only in Stockinette Stitch, it is not necessary to move the marker after every round. The marker only needs to mark the first needle so you can stop after the third needle when it's time to work the Bottom Border.

Remove the marker and place it around the first stitch to indicate the beginning of the round. The Bottom Border is worked in Garter Stitch, same as the Top Border.

Rnd 1: Purl across each needle.

Rnd 2: Knit across each needle.

Rnds 3-8: Repeat Rnds 1 and 2, 3 times.

3-Needle Bind Off

🎥 A 3-needle bind off is a way to bind off while forming the bottom seam. You first need to move the stitches onto two needles. Slip the first 4 sts from the second needle onto the first needle and the remaining 4 sts onto the third needle, having 12 sts on each of 2 needles. Hold the needles parallel to each other *(Fig. 7a)*. Remove the marker from the first stitch.

Fig. 7a

Insert an empty needle as if to **knit** into the first st on the front needle **and** into the first st on the back needle *(Fig. 7b)*. Knit these 2 sts together and slip them off the left needles.

Fig. 7b

★ Knit the next st on each needle together and slip them off the left needles. To bind off, insert one of the left needles into the first st on the right needle and bring the first st over the second st and off the right needle; repeat from ★ across until all of the sts have been bound off; cut the yarn and pull the end through the loop.

Using 2 Double Pointed Needles
CORD

Cords are easy to knit in the round using the I-cord technique, which only uses 2 double pointed needles.

🎥 **To make an I-cord**, cast on 3 sts.

★ Without turning the needle, slide the sts to the opposite end of the needle; holding the working yarn with a tight tension **behind** the work, K3 *(Fig. 8a)*.

Fig. 8a

Repeat from ★ until the Cord measures approximately 12" (30.5 cm) from cast on edge, giving the Cord a gentle tug every few rnds to close the gap between the first and last sts *(Fig. 8b)*.

Fig. 8b

Without turning the needle, slide the sts to the opposite end of the needle and bind off all stitches leaving a long end for sewing.

Using the long end on the Cord, weave the Cord through the Eyelet Row of the Pouch; sew the ends of the Cord together.

GOOD JOB!!!
You completed your first project knitting
in the round on double pointed needles.

BABY HAT

Beginning at the center of the crown, this little hat gradually adds stitches until it's time to work a simple lace pattern. A section of ribbing finishes it off.

 **EASY**

Finished Measurement: 14¹/₂" (37 cm) circumference

SHOPPING LIST

Yarn (Light Weight)
[5 ounces, 459 yards
(141 grams, 420 meters) per skein]:
☐ 1 skein

Knitting Needles
☐ 7-8" (18-20.5 cm) Double pointed (set of 5),
size 5 (3.75 mm) **or** size needed for gauge

Additional Supplies
☐ Split ring marker

GAUGE INFORMATION
In Stockinette Stitch, 22 sts and 29 rows/rnds = 4" (10 cm)

TECHNIQUES USED
YO *(Fig. 16a, page 42)*
Increases - Kf&b *(Figs. 17a & b, page 43)*
K2 tog *(Fig. 22, page 45)*
SSK *(Figs. 24a-c, page 45)*
Slip 2, K1, P2SSO *(Figs. 27a & b, page 46)*

INSTRUCTIONS
Beginning at the Center
SHAPING

Rnd 1: Beginning at the center, make a slip knot and place it on a double pointed needle; Kf&b of the slip knot twice: 4 sts.

Rnd 2: Without turning the needle, slide the sts to the opposite end of the needle; holding the working yarn with a tight tension **behind** the work when working the first st, Kf&b of each st across: 8 sts.

Divide sts onto 4 needles, placing 2 sts on each needle and form a square with the needles *(Fig. 9)*.

Fig. 9

Rnd 3: K1, place a split ring marker around the st just worked to indicate the beginning of the round *(see Markers, page 41)*, knit around.

Rnd 4: Kf&b of each st around: 4 sts on each needle for a total of 16 sts.

Rnd 5: Knit around.

Rnd 6: (Kf&b, K1) around: 6 sts on each needle for a total of 24 sts.

Rnd 7: Knit around.

Rnd 8: (Kf&b, K2) around: 8 sts on each needle for a total of 32 sts.

Rnd 9: Knit around.

Rnd 10: (Kf&b, K3) around: 10 sts on each needle for a total of 40 sts.

Rnd 11: Knit around.

Rnd 12: (Kf&b, K4) around: 12 sts on each needle for a total of 48 sts.

Rnd 13: Knit around.

Rnd 14: (Kf&b, K5) around: 14 sts on each needle for a total of 56 sts.

Rnd 15: Knit around.

Rnd 16: (Kf&b, K6) around: 16 sts on each needle for a total of 64 sts.

Rnd 17: Knit around.

Rnd 18: (Kf&b, K7) around: 18 sts on each needle for a total of 72 sts.

Rnd 19: Knit around.

Rnd 20: (Kf&b, K8) around: 20 sts on each needle for a total of 80 sts.

BODY

Knit every rnd until Hat measures approximately 5" (12.5 cm) from center.

LACE PATTERN

Rearrange stitches for ease in working the lace pattern as follows: 16 sts on first needle, 24 sts on second needle, 16 sts on third needle, and 24 sts on fourth needle. You will be able to work the lace pattern twice across the needles with 16 sts and 3 times across the needles with 24 sts.

Rnd 1: K2, SSK, YO, K1, YO, K2 tog, ★ K3, SSK, YO, K1, YO, K2 tog; repeat from ★ around to last st, K1.

Rnd 2: Knit around.

Rnd 3: K2, YO, slip 2, K1, P2SSO, YO, ★ K5, YO, slip 2, K1, P2SSO, YO; repeat from ★ around to last 3 sts, K3.

Rnd 4: Knit around.

Rnd 5: K2, SSK, YO, K1, YO, K2 tog, ★ K3, SSK, YO, K1, YO, K2 tog; repeat from ★ around to last st, K1.

Rnds 6-10: Knit around.

RIBBING

Rnds 1-8: (K1, P1) around.

Bind off all sts **loosely** in ribbing.

We've created bonus videos for you @ www.leisurearts.com/6342

Take a look!

FINGERLESS MITTS

Use the techniques you've learned so far to make a pair of stylish mitts. The thumb hole is made by binding off stitches and then adding them back on. There are no seams to sew!

▮▮▯▭ **EASY +**

Finished Size: 7" circumference x 8½" high (18 cm x 21.5 cm)

SHOPPING LIST

Yarn (Medium Weight)
[2.5 ounces, 121 yards
(70 grams, 111 meters) per skein]:

☐ 1 skein

Knitting Needles

☐ 5" (12.5 cm) Double pointed (set of 5),
size 8 (5 mm) **or** size needed for gauge

Additional Supplies

☐ Split ring marker

GAUGE INFORMATION

In pattern, 2 repeats (8 sts) and 12 rows/rnds = 1³/₄"
 (4.5 cm)

Gauge Swatch: 3" (7.5 cm) wide

Cast on 14 sts.

Row 1: Knit across.

Row 2: Purl across.

Row 3: K1, ★ with yarn in **back**, slip 1 as if to **knit**, K3, PSSO3 *(Fig. 10, page 30)*; repeat from ★ across to last st, K1: 11 sts.

Row 4: P4, YO, (P3, YO) twice, P1: 14 sts.

Rows 5-8: Repeat Rows 1-4.

Bind off all sts.

TECHNIQUES USED

▰ YO *(Fig. 16a, page 42)*
▰ YO twice *(Fig. 16c, page 43)*
▰ Kf&b *(Figs. 17a & b, page 43)*
▰ K2 tog *(Fig. 22, page 45)*

STITCH GUIDE

PASS SLIPPED STITCH OVER 3 STITCHES
(abbreviated PSSO3)

Pass slipped st over 3 sts just made and off needle *(Fig. 10)*.

Fig. 10

INSTRUCTIONS
BOTTOM RIBBING

Cast on 33 sts.

Divide sts onto 4 needles, placing 8 sts on the first 3 needles and 9 sts on the last needle; then form a square keeping the cast on ridge straight *(Fig. 11)*.

Fig. 11

Rnd 1 (Right side): Slip last st made onto the first needle, knit the last st and the first st together to join the round, **place a split ring marker** around the st just made to indicate the beginning of the round *(see Markers, page 41)*, K1, P2, (K2, P2) around: 32 sts.

Rnds 2-11: (K2, P2) around.

BODY

Rnds 1 and 2: Knit around.

Rnd 3: ★ Slip 1 as if to **knit**, K3, PSSO3; repeat from ★ around: 24 sts.

Rnd 4: (YO, K3) around: 32 sts.

Rnds 5-20: Repeat Rnds 1-4, 4 times.

Rnd 21: Bind off 4 sts for thumb opening, knit around: 28 sts.

Rnd 22: YO twice, knit around: 30 sts.

Rnd 23: Slip first YO off needle to form a large loop on left needle and Kf&b twice in loop; ★ slip 1 as if to **knit**, K3, PSSO3; repeat from ★ around: 25 sts.

Rnd 24: K4, (YO, K3) around: 32 sts.

Rnds 25-30: Repeat Rnds 1-4 once, then repeat Rnds 1 and 2 once **more**.

TOP RIBBING
Rnds 1-6: (K2, P2) around.

Bind off all sts **loosely** in ribbing.

THUMB
With **right** side facing, **pick up 12 sts** evenly spaced around thumb opening *(Figs. 30a & b, page 47)*, placing 3 sts on each of 4 needles.

Rnds 1-4: (K2, P2) around.

Bind off all sts **loosely** in ribbing.

COMBINING TECHNIQUES

Sometimes you'll need to use both double pointed needles and circular needles in the same project.

The Family Hat on page 32 begins at the bottom edge, requiring a circular needle. As the stitches are decreased for the Shaping, you will get to the point when there will be too few stitches to fit on the circular needle and double pointed needles will be needed.

The Baby Blanket on page 35 begins at the center, requiring double pointed needles. As stitches are increased, there will soon be too many stitches to comfortably use double pointed needles and a circular needle will be needed.

To change from a circular needle to 4 double pointed needles, slip one fourth of the stitches from the circular needle onto each of 4 double pointed needles purlwise as specified in the instructions **or** work the next round using a new empty needle for each section of the stitches, so that the stitches are divided evenly onto 4 separate needles at the end of the round.

To change from double pointed needles to a circular needle, work the next round with the circular needle called for in the Shopping List **or** slip all of the stitches purlwise from the double pointed needles onto the circular needle before beginning the next round.

FAMILY HAT

◼️◼️◻️◻️ **EASY**

Use both circular and double pointed needles to make this hat, which comes in sizes for everyone in your family.

——— SHOPPING LIST ———

Yarn (Medium Weight)

**[5 ounces, 256 yards
(141 grams, 234 meters) per skein]:**

☐ 1 skein

Knitting Needles

☐ 16" (40.5 cm) Circular, size 8 (5 mm)
or size needed for gauge
☐ 7-8" (18-20.5 cm) Double pointed (set of 5),
size 8 (5 mm) **or** size needed for gauge

Additional Supplies

☐ Split ring marker
☐ Yarn needle

SIZE INFORMATION

Sizes	Finished Circumference
Child's	18¹/₄" (46.5 cm)
Woman's	19¹/₄" (49 cm)
Man's	21¹/₄" (54 cm)

Size Note: We have printed the instructions for the sizes in different colors to make it easier for you to find:

· Child's size in Blue
· Woman's size in Pink
· Man's size in Green
Instructions in black apply to all sizes.

GAUGE INFORMATION

In Stockinette Stitch, 16 sts and 22 rnds = 4" (10 cm)

TECHNIQUE USED

🎥 K2 tog *(Fig. 22, page 45)*

INSTRUCTIONS
Using a Circular Needle
RIBBING

Using circular needle, cast on 73{77-85} sts.

🎥 Place a marker on the right hand point to indicate the beginning of the round *(see Markers, page 41)*.
🎥 Begin working in rounds *(Figs. 2 & 3, page 8)*.

Rnd 1 (Right side)**:** (K2, P2) around to last st, K1.

Rnd 2: K1, (P2, K2) around.

Rnd 3: (P2, K2) around to last st, P1.

Rnd 4: P1, (K2, P2) around.

Repeat Rnds 1-4 for pattern until Ribbing measures approximately 2{2-3}"/5{5-7.5} cm from cast on edge.

BODY

Knit each round until piece measures approximately 4{5-5½}"/10{12.5-14} cm from cast on edge.

SHAPING

Man's Size Only

Rnd 1: (K 15, K2 tog) around: 80 sts.

Rnd 2: Knit around.

Rnd 3: (K8, K2 tog) around: 72 sts.

Rnd 4: Knit around.

Using Double Pointed Needles

It's time to change to double pointed needles to complete the Shaping. ▶ Dividing sts onto 4 needles *(Fig. 11, page 30)*, slip 18 sts as if to **purl** onto each of 4 needles **or** work the next round using a new empty needle for each fourth of the stitches, so that there are 18 sts on 4 separate needles at the end of the round.

Rnd 5: (K7, K2 tog) around: 64 sts.

Rnd 6: Knit around.

Rnd 7: (K6, K2 tog) around: 56 sts.

Rnd 8: Knit around.

Rnd 9: (K5, K2 tog) around: 48 sts.

Rnd 10: Knit around.

Rnd 11: (K4, K2 tog) around: 40 sts.

Rnd 12: Knit around.

Rnd 13: (K3, K2 tog) around: 32 sts.

Rnd 14: Knit around.

Rnd 15: (K2, K2 tog) around: 24 sts.

Rnd 16: Knit around.

Rnd 17: (K1, K2 tog) around: 16 sts.

Rnd 18: Knit around.

Rnd 19: K2 tog around: 8 sts.

▶ To gather the stitches, cut the yarn leaving a long end for sewing. Thread the yarn needle with the end and slip the remaining sts onto the yarn needle and yarn; pull tightly to close and secure end.

Woman's Size Only

Rnd 1: K2, (K2 tog, K 13) around: 72 sts.

Work same as Man's Hat beginning with Rnd 4 of Shaping.

Child's Size Only

Rnd 1: K2 tog, knit around: 72 sts.

Work same as Man's Hat beginning with Rnd 4 of Shaping.

BABY BLANKET

■■■□ **INTERMEDIATE**

Start this blanket in the center using double pointed needles and just 12 stitches. As you continue knitting more rounds and increasing the number of stitches, you will need to change to a circular needle with a 16" cable, then a 24" cable, and eventually a 36" cable.

Finished Size: 31" (78.5 cm) diameter

SHOPPING LIST

Yarn (Light Weight)

[5 ounces, 358 yards
(141 grams, 328 meters) per skein]:

☐ Color A (White) - 2 skeins

[4 ounces, 242 yards
(113 grams, 222 meters) per skein]:

☐ Color B (Ombre) - 2 skeins

Knitting Needles

☐ 7-8" (18-20.5 cm) Double pointed (set of 5),
size 5 (3.75 mm) **or** size needed for gauge

☐ Circular, size 5 (3.75 mm):
16" (40.5 cm), 24" (61 cm), **and** 36" (91.5 cm)
or size needed for gauge

Additional Supplies

☐ Ring markers - 6

☐ Split ring marker

☐ Tapestry needle

GAUGE INFORMATION

In K2, P2 ribbing, 24 sts and 23 rnds = 4" (10 cm)

TECHNIQUE USED

YO **(Figs. 16a & b, pages 42 & 43)**

Increases - Kf&b **(Figs. 17a & b, page 43)**

Increases - Pb&f **(Fig. 18, page 43)**

INSTRUCTIONS
Adjustable Loop

The Blanket begins at the center using double pointed needles. An adjustable loop allows many stitches to be cast on without leaving a large hole at the center of the project.

To cast on sts using an adjustable loop, using Color A, drape the working yarn around your index finger and hold it in your hand, then make a loop and hold it with your thumb and second finger *(Fig. 12a)*.

Fig. 12a

Insert your needle under the working yarn from **right** to **left**, then through the loop you are holding from **front** to **back** *(Figs. 12b & c)*, place needle over the working yarn and bring it back through the loop *(Fig. 12d)* (2 sts on needle).

Fig. 12b

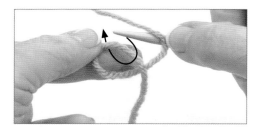

Fig. 12c

Fig. 12d

★ Bring the yarn over your needle from **front** to **back** *(Fig. 12e)*, then insert your needle through the loop you are holding **front** to **back** *(Fig. 12f)*, place the needle over the working yarn and bring it back through the loop *(Fig. 12g)* (2 more sts on the needle).

Fig. 12e

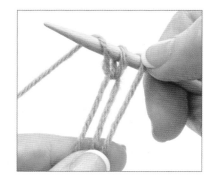

Fig. 12f

Fig. 12g

Repeat from ★ 4 times **more** for a total of 12 sts *(Fig. 12h)*.

Fig. 12h

Working in the Round

Instead of slipping the stitches onto separate needles, Rnd 1 begins by working across the cast on stitches, changing to using a new empty needle after every 3 stitches, so that the stitches are divided onto 4 separate needles at the end of the round.

As you start working with an empty needle, the previous needles can just dangle, or they can be held with your left hand *(Figs. 5c & d, page 20)*.

Rnd 1 (Right side)**: Turn;** 🎥 place a split ring marker around the first st to indicate the beginning of the rnd *(see Markers, page 41)*, (K1, P1) across placing 3 sts on each of 4 needles *(Fig. 13a)*.

Fig. 13a

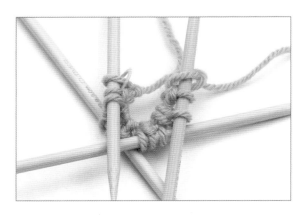

With the **right** side toward you, 🎥 form a square with the 4 needles *(Fig. 13b)*.

Fig. 13b

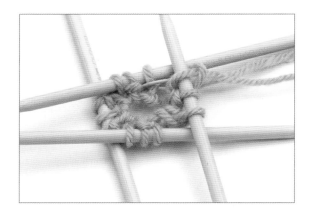

Pull the beginning yarn end to tighten the loop *(Fig. 13c)*. If it loosens up as you work, just tighten it again; it will be secured later.

Fig. 13c

Note: You will work in the same manner as for the Pouch on page 17.

Slide the stitches to the center of each needle when not in use. When you are ready to work across a needle, slide the stitches to the tip, then back to the center of their new needle after all of the stitches are worked.

At the beginning of each round, move the marker to the new stitch after the first stitch has been worked.

Continue working the first stitch of each needle firmly to prevent gaps and the ladder effect *(Fig. 6, page 21)*.

Rnd 2 (Right side)**:** Do **not** turn; (Kf&b, Pb&f) around: 6 sts on each needle for a total of 24 sts.

Rnd 3: (K2, P2) around.

Rnd 4: ★ (Kf&b, P) all in next st, (P, Kf&b) all in next st, P2; repeat from ★ around: 12 sts on each needle for a total of 48 sts.

Rnds 5-7: (K2, P2) around.

Rnd 8: ★ K2, (Pb&f, K) all in next st, (K, Pb&f) all in next st, K2, P2; repeat from ★ around: 18 sts on each needle for a total of 72 sts.

Rnds 9-11: (K2, P2) around.

Rnd 12: K2, P2, (Kf&b, P) all in next st, (P, Kf&b) all in next st, P2, ★ (K2, P2) twice, (Kf&b, P) all in next st, (P, Kf&b) all in next st, P2; repeat from ★ 4 times **more**, K2, P2: 24 sts on each needle for a total of 96 sts.

Rnds 13-15: (K2, P2) around.

On the next round, place markers as instructed to mark placement of increases in the following rounds.

Rnd 16: K2, P2, K2, (Pb&f, K) all in next st, place marker, (K, Pb&f) all in next st, ★ K2, (P2, K2) 3 times, (Pb&f, K) all in next st, place marker, (K, Pb&f) all in next st; repeat from ★ 4 times **more**, (K2, P2) twice: 30 sts on each needle for a total of 120 sts.

Change to a 16" (40.5 cm) circular needle when there are too many stitches to comfortably knit with double pointed needles *(see Combining Techniques, page 31)*. Change to a 24" (61 cm) circular needle, then a 36" (91.5 cm) circular needle when stitches become crowded.

Slip markers from the left needle to the right needle when you come to them.

Rnds 17-19: (K2, P2) around.

Rnd 20: (K2, P2) across to within one st of next marker, (Kf&b, P) all in next st, (P, Kf&b) all in next st, P2, ★ (K2, P2) across to within one st of next marker, (Kf&b, P) all in next st, (P, Kf&b) all in next st, P2; repeat from ★ 4 times **more**, (K2, P2) across: 144 sts.

Rnds 21-23: (K2, P2) around.

Rnd 24: K2, (P2, K2) across to within one st of next marker, (Pb&f, K) all in next st, (K, Pb&f) all in next st, ★ K2, (P2, K2) across to within one st of next marker, (Pb&f, K) all in next st, (K, Pb&f) all in next st; repeat from ★ 4 times **more**, (K2, P2) across: 168 sts.

Rnds 25-64: Repeat Rnds 17-24, 5 times: 408 sts.

Leaving the marker indicating the beginning of the round, remove all remaining markers as you work the next round.

Rnd 65: Cut Color A; with Color B, ★ K1, YO, K1, P1, YO, P1; repeat from ★ around: 612 sts.

Rnd 66: ★ K1, Kf&b, K1, P1, Pb&f, P1; repeat from ★ around: 816 sts.

Rnds 67-89: (K4, P4) around.

Bind off all sts in ribbing.

Pull the beginning yarn end to make sure the center is closed. Using a tapestry needle, secure the end, and weave it in.

GENERAL INSTRUCTIONS

ABBREVIATIONS

cm	centimeters
K	knit
K&P	knit and purl
Kf&b	knit in front & back
mm	millimeters
P	purl
P&K	purl and knit
Pb&f	purl in back & front
PSSO	pass slipped stitch over
PSSO3	pass slipped stitch over 3
P2SSO	pass 2 slipped stitches over
Rnd(s)	Round(s)
SSK	slip, slip, knit
st(s)	stitch(es)
tog	together
YO	yarn over

KNIT TERMINOLOGY

UNITED STATES	INTERNATIONAL
gauge =	tension
bind off =	cast off
yarn over (YO) =	yarn forward (yfwd) **or**
	yarn around needle (yrn)

SYMBOLS & TERMS

★ — work instructions following ★ as many **more** times as indicated in addition to the first time.

( ) or [ ] — work enclosed instructions **as many** times as specified by the number immediately following **or** work all enclosed instructions in the stitch or space indicated **or** contains explanatory remarks.

colon (:) — the number(s) given after a colon at the end of a round or row denote(s) the number of stitches you should have on that round or row.

GAUGE

Exact gauge is **essential** for proper size or fit. Before beginning your project, make a sample swatch in the yarn and needle specified in the individual instructions. After completing the swatch, measure it, counting your stitches and rows carefully. If your swatch is larger or smaller than specified, **make another, changing needle size to get the correct gauge.** Keep trying until you find the size needles that will give you the specified gauge.

Yarn Weight Symbol & Names	LACE 0	SUPER FINE 1	FINE 2	LIGHT 3	MEDIUM 4	BULKY 5	SUPER BULKY 6
Type of Yarns in Category	Fingering, size 10 crochet thread	Sock, Fingering, Baby	Sport, Baby	DK, Light Worsted	Worsted, Afghan, Aran	Chunky, Craft, Rug	Bulky, Roving
Knit Gauge Range* in Stockinette St to 4" (10 cm)	33-40** sts	27-32 sts	23-26 sts	21-24 sts	16-20 sts	12-15 sts	6-11 sts
Advised Needle Size Range	000-1	1 to 3	3 to 5	5 to 7	7 to 9	9 to 11	11 and larger

*GUIDELINES ONLY: The chart above reflects the most commonly used gauges and needle sizes for specific yarn categories.

** Lace weight yarns are usually knitted on larger needles to create lacy openwork patterns. Accordingly, a gauge range is difficult to determine. Always follow the gauge stated in your pattern.

■□□□ **BEGINNER**		Projects for first-time knitters using basic knit and purl stitches. Minimal shaping.
■■□□ **EASY**		Projects using basic stitches, repetitive stitch patterns, simple color changes, and simple shaping and finishing.
■■■□ **INTERMEDIATE**		Projects with a variety of stitches, such as basic cables and lace, simple intarsia, double-pointed needles and knitting in the round needle techniques, mid-level shaping and finishing.
■■■■ **EXPERIENCED**		Projects using advanced techniques and stitches, such as short rows, fair isle, more intricate intarsia, cables, lace patterns, and numerous color changes.

MARKERS

As a convenience to you, we have used markers to help distinguish the beginning of a round and to mark the placement of increases in the blanket. You may use purchased markers or a length of contrasting color yarn. Place markers as instructed.

Circular Needle

A ring marker, split ring marker, or a loop of a contrasting color scrap yarn can be used to indicate the beginning of the round. It should be placed **before** the first stitch *(Figs. 14a & b)*. When you reach a marker on each round, slip it from the left needle tip to the right needle tip; remove it when no longer needed.

Fig. 14a

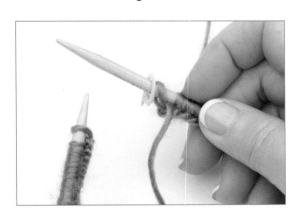

Fig. 14b

Double Pointed Needles

A split ring marker can be used to indicate the beginning of the round when using double pointed needles. Place the marker around the first stitch on the first needle *(Fig. 5b, page 20)*. At the beginning of each round, move the marker to a new stitch after the first stitch has been worked. Remove the marker when no longer needed.

A ring marker or a loop of scrap yarn can be used to indicate the first needle, but it should be placed **after** the first stitch so it won't slide off the needle *(Fig. 14c)*. Just remember that the first stitch on that needle is the beginning of the round. When you reach a marker on each round, slip it from the left needle to the right needle; remove it when no longer needed.

Fig. 14c

The yarn end hangs between the first and last needle *(Fig. 14d)* and can be used to indicate the first needle instead of placing a marker. If the project is worked even in Stockinette Stitch, this can be easier than moving a marker every round.

Fig. 14d

ADDING NEW STITCHES

Insert the right needle into stitch as if to **knit**, yarn over and pull loop through *(Fig. 15a)*, insert the left needle into the loop just worked from **front** to **back** and slip the loop onto the left needle *(Fig. 15b)*. Repeat for required number of stitches.

Fig. 15a

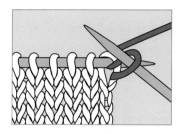

Fig. 15b

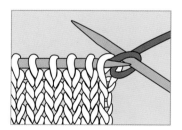

YARN OVERS

A yarn over *(abbreviated YO)* is simply placing the yarn over the right needle creating an extra stitch. The yarn over produces a hole in the knit fabric and it can be used for a lacy effect or to increase stitches. On the row following a yarn over, you must be careful to keep it on the needle and treat it as a stitch by knitting or purling it as instructed.

To make a yarn over, you'll loop the yarn over the needle like you would to knit or purl a stitch, bringing it either to the front or the back of the piece so that it'll be ready to work the next stitch, creating a new stitch on the needle as follows:

After a Knit Stitch, Before a Knit Stitch

Bring the yarn forward **between** the needles, then back **over** the top of the right hand needle, so that it is now in position to knit the next stitch *(Fig. 16a)*.

Fig. 16a

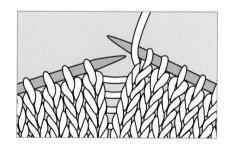

KNITTING NEEDLES CONVERSION CHART																			
U.S.	0	1	2	3	4	5	6	7	8	9	10	10½	11	13	15	17	19	35	50
U.K.	13	12	11	10	9	8	7	6	5	4	3	2	1	00	000	---	---	---	---
Metric - mm	2	2.25	2.75	3.25	3.5	3.75	4	4.5	5	5.5	6	6.5	8	9	10	12.75	15	19	25

After a Purl Stitch, Before a Purl Stitch

Take the yarn over the right hand needle to the back, then forward under it, so that it is now in position to purl the next stitch *(Fig. 16b)*.

Fig. 16b

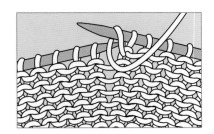

Yarn Over Twice *(abbreviated YO twice)*

★ Bring the yarn forward **between** the needles, then back **over** the top of the right hand needle; repeat from ★ once **more**, so that it is now in position to knit the next stitch *(Fig. 16c)*.

Fig. 16c

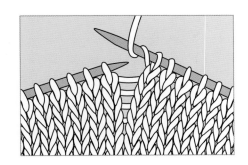

INCREASES

The increases in this book use one stitch to make two or more stitches. The type of increase used depends on the stitch needed to maintain the pattern.

Knit in front & back
(abbreviated Kf&b)

Knit the next stitch but do **not** slip the old stitch off the left needle *(Fig. 17a)*. Insert the right needle into the **back** loop of the **same** stitch and knit it *(Fig. 17b)*, then slip the old stitch off the left needle.

Fig. 17a   **Fig. 17b**

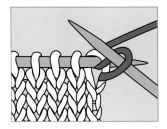 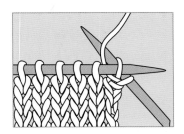

Purl in back & front *(abbreviated Pb&f)*

Purl the next stitch in the **back** loop *(Fig. 18)* but do **not** slip the old stitch off the left needle. Insert the right needle into the front loop of the **same** stitch and purl it. Slip the old stitch off the left needle.

Fig. 18

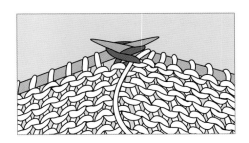

Combination Increases

Many stitches can be made from one stitch. Work as many stitches as indicated all in the same stitch.

Knit and Purl (abbreviated K&P)

Knit the next stitch but do **not** slip the old stitch off the left needle. With yarn in front, insert the right needle in the front loop of the **same** stitch (Fig. 19) and purl it. Slip the old stitch off the left needle.

Fig. 19

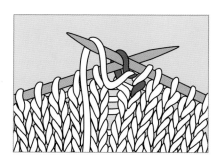

Purl and Knit (abbreviated P&K)

Purl the next stitch but do **not** slip the old stitch off the left needle. With yarn in back, insert the right needle in the front loop of the **same** stitch (Fig. 20) and knit it. Slip the old stitch off the left needle.

Fig. 20

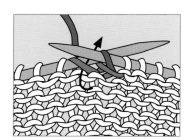

(Knit, Yarn Over, Knit) All In Next Stitch
[abbreviated (K, YO, K) all in next st]

Knit the next stitch but do **not** slip the old stitch off the left needle, YO (Fig. 21), knit the **same** stitch, then slip the old stitch off the left needle.

Fig. 21

DECREASES
Knit 2 Together *(abbreviated K2 tog)*

Insert the right needle into the **front** of the first two stitches on the left needle as if to **knit** *(Fig. 22)*, then **knit** them together as if they were one stitch.

Fig. 22

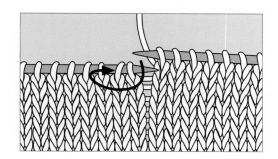

Knit 3 Together *(abbreviated K3 tog)*

Insert the right needle into the **front** of the first three stitches on the left needle as if to **knit** *(Fig. 23)*, then **knit** them together as if they were one stitch.

Fig. 23

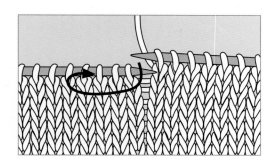

Slip, Slip, Knit *(abbreviated SSK)*

Separately slip two stitches as if to **knit** *(Fig. 24a)*. Insert the **left** needle into the **front** of both slipped stitches *(Fig. 24b)* and then **knit** them together as if they were one stitch *(Fig. 24c)*.

Fig. 24a

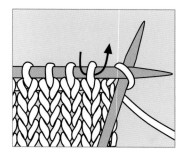

Fig. 24b

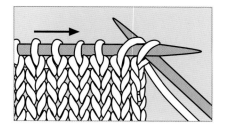

Fig. 24c

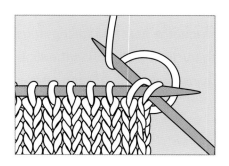

Slip 1, Knit 1, Pass Slipped Stitch Over *(abbreviated slip 1, K1, PSSO)*

With yarn in back, slip one stitch as if to **knit** *(Fig. 25a)*. Knit the next stitch. With the left needle, bring the slipped stitch over the knit stitch *(Fig. 25b)* and off the needle.

Fig. 25a

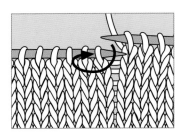

Fig. 25b

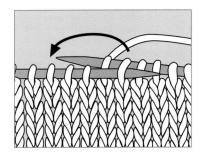

Slip 1, Knit 2 Together, Pass Slipped Stitch Over *(abbreviated slip 1, K2 tog, PSSO)*

With yarn in back, slip one stitch as if to **knit** *(Fig. 25a, page 46)*, then knit the next two stitches together *(Fig. 23, page 45)*. With the left needle, bring the slipped stitch over the stitch just made *(Fig. 26)* and off the needle.

Fig. 26

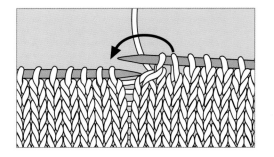

Slip 2, Knit 1, Pass 2 Slipped Stitches Over *(abbreviated slip 2, K1, P2SSO)*

With yarn in back, slip two stitches together as if to **knit** *(Fig. 27a)*, then knit the next stitch. With the left needle, bring both slipped stitches over the knit stitch *(Fig. 27b)* and off the needle.

Fig. 27a

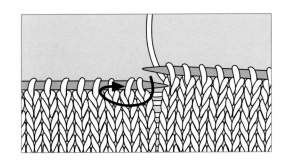

Fig. 27b

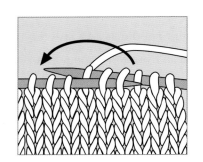

Purl 2 Together *(abbreviated P2 tog)*

Insert the right needle into the **front** of the first two stitches on the left needle as if to **purl** *(Fig. 28)*, then **purl** them together as if they were one stitch.

Fig. 28

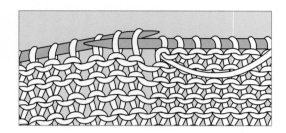

Purl 3 Together *(abbreviated P3 tog)*

Insert the right needle into the **front** of the first three stitches on the left needle as if to **purl** *(Fig. 29)*, then **purl** them together as if they were one stitch.

Fig. 29

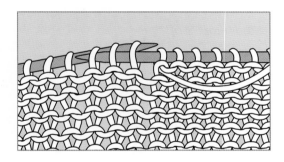

PICKING UP STITCHES

When instructed to pick up stitches, insert the needle from the **front** to the **back** under two strands at the edge of the worked piece *(Figs. 30a & b)*. Put the yarn around the needle as if to **knit**, then bring the needle with the yarn back through the stitch to the right side, resulting in a stitch on the needle.

Repeat this along the edge, picking up the required number of stitches.

A crochet hook may be helpful to pull yarn through.

Fig. 30a

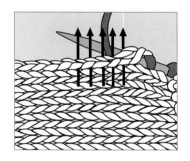

Fig. 30b

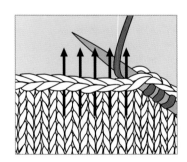

YARN INFORMATION

The projects in this book were made using a variety of yarns. Any brand in the specific weight yarn may be used. It is best to refer to the yardage/meters when determining how many skeins or balls to purchase. Remember, to arrive at the finished size, it is the GAUGE/TENSION that is important, not the brand of yarn.

For your convenience, listed below are the yarns used to create our photography models.

HEADBAND
Red Heart® Boutique Unforgettable™
#3960 Tidal

COWL
Bernat® Softee® Chunky™
Main Color - #29440 Spirited
Contrasting Color - #28440 Beetroot

LACE CAPELET
Patons® Lace™
#33302 Mystic Teal

POUCH
Lion Brand® Heartland® Tweed
#373 Everglades Tweed

BABY HAT
Lion Brand® Baby Soft®
#143 Lavender

FINGERLESS MITTS
Lion Brand® Vanna's Choice®
#500 Patchwork Grey

FAMILY HAT
Red Heart® Soft®
#4608 Wine

BABY BLANKET
Red Heart® Baby TLC™
Color A: #5011 White
Color B: #5950 Miami